MY LITTLE PRAYER BOOK

75 PRAYERS, POEMS & MANTRAS FOR ILLUMINATION

ANNIE VAZQUEZ

1st Edition | 01
Hardcover ISBN: 979-8-9869891-0-5

First Published November 2023

Also available in:
Paperback: 979-8-9862106-8-1

For inquiries and bulk orders, please email:
indieearthpublishinghouse@gmail.com

Printed in the United States of America   1 2 3 4 5 6 7 8 9

Indie Earth Publishing Inc.
| Miami, FL |

www.indieearthbooks.com

Praise for *My Little Prayer Book:*
75 Prayers, Poems and Mantras for Illumination

"A harmony of prayer and poetry, *My Little Prayer Book* empowers the reader with just the right words to seek guidance during all of life's varied moments. Annie Vazquez is a gifted teacher, and her warmth and wisdom comes through on every page. Keep this encouraging volume nearby to turn to again and again."
— Alejandra Ramos, Host of Good Morning America

"Annie Vazquez's *My Little Prayer Book* immediately filled me with peace and comfort that I am always divinely guided and protected. She provides us with a toolkit of beautiful words that have the power to call in abundance, protection, love, support and miracles into our lives. This is a book that will be on my nightstand as a reminder that I always have access to the divine to create my own reality via prayers and words of manifestation."
— Ana Flores, Founder and CEO of We All Grow Latina

"At a moment in time when we are relentlessly bombarded by negativity, fear and doubt in the news and on social media, Annie has crafted a much-needed guidebook to help us set positive intentions and manage our self-speak. Her uncomplicated writings provide readers with accessible tools for making purposeful asks from the Universe, but also with words to share with friends and family that might need encouragement through a variety of challenges."
— Alex Traverzo, Director of Integrated Marketing at HOLA!

"Annie Vazquez's *My Little Prayer Book* is so needed and vital today—a diverse, memorable and inspiring collection of prayers and mantras for all walks of life. I've had the pleasure of knowing Annie for over 20 years, and her empathy and talent continue to inspire and spread goodwill. A great gift for anyone in your life looking for a spiritual boost."
— Alex Segura, Bestselling Author of *Secret Identity*

"*My Little Prayer Book* is a much-needed spiritual guide for those seeking clarity and connection with the divine. In the midst of our digital age, where distractions are abound, the timeless power of mantras and prayers is an anchor. This toolkit is an essential resource for anyone navigating the journey of self-discovery and spiritual fulfillment."
— Suanny Garcia, Author of *The New Latina*

"When you create from a place of love, you make magic. *My Little Prayer Book* is a thoughtfully-curated mystical gem we can all benefit and learn from. For me, it's one of Annie's greatest gifts to the world."
— Valerie Mesa, Intuitive Astrologer, Stylecaster Writer and Visual Storyteller

"*My Little Prayer Book* is a beautiful, easy-to-read guide that welcomes all readers, no matter their religious, secular or spiritual backgrounds. Its poetic prayers are filled with heartfelt requests for good news, good karma and abundance, offering a lyrical approach to manifesting the life of your dreams. Annie's book ensures that no one is forgotten."
— Allison Ramirez, Lonely Planet + Food & Drink Journalist

"Annie Vazquez's *My Little Prayer Book* does exactly what Annie has been doing for years; it digs deep into your soul and reminds you that you are loved. Annie has figured out a way to make a cheat sheet for prayers, and that is something we can all use. I've said this before and I'll say it again... Annie is Miami's Jedi."

— Lucy Lopez, Host of The Mamacita Rica Podcast

"Divine perfection and timing within words. As I dove page by page, effortless tears ran down as I ingested depth in its simplest form. A complete full-circle book of prayers and poems for the soul! Exactly what I needed to come across, and of course, it presented itself in divine timing. Thank you, Annie, for being a vessel of love and light in this journey. It's an honor crossing paths with angels on earth like you but a bigger honor to call you an angel and a friend!"

— Jo' Martinez, Creatrix of Despojitos MIAMI

"*My Little Prayer Book* is perfect for anyone who is looking to connect to the power of prayer. Whether you're a beginner and praying is something you're starting to explore, or you've prayed every day, the way Annie shares her words makes them accessible to people of all ages and backgrounds. Not only is it beautifully written, it is laid out in a user-friendly and inviting way. *My Little Prayer Book* is a gift Annie gives to the world so we can believe in and experience the power of prayer. Her writing teaches us that our words and thoughts are powerful, and her work inspires readers to ask for and be ready to receive what the Universe has to offer."

— Diana Limongi, Host of Parenting and Politics Podcast

"If you've been looking for a sign to connect with yourself spiritually, look no further than *My Little Prayer Book*. Annie has created a wonderful guide to prayer, offering poetry, angel numbers, mantras and all we need to develop better relationships with ourselves, those around us and the Universe itself. *My Little Prayer Book* is something you'll want to keep close by so you can return to it time and time again."

— Flor Ana, Author of *The Truth About Love*

"Annie Vazquez has taken her love of others and crafted a Rosetta Stone to help readers communicate with their inner selves. *My Little Prayer Book* allows readers to immerse themselves in poetry, releasing blocks as they ask the universe—and in turn, themselves—for guidance. A work like this can only be born out of love and self-work, and this is the type of book that is sorely needed in a world that becomes more and more divided; it is a reminder that we have more in common than we realize."

— Renzo Del Castillo, Author of *Still*

"This little prayer book is a gem, a blessing and a gift to us all. It is beautiful to be able to reach for this book in times of need, in moments of gratitude and simply for no reason at all. We needed this, and I am eternally grateful for Annie's devotion to loving herself and humanity enough to share it."

— Nicole Rodriguez, Yoga Instructor

"I love this compilation of pick-me-ups, daily reminders and reassurance. I cannot wait to use these prayers and mantras in my daily self-care and spiritual rituals. The book has such a positive light energy to it."

— Rebecca Arroyo, Therapist and Yoga Instructor

My Little Prayer Book

75 Prayers, Poems & Mantras
for Illumination

Written by Annie Vazquez

Illustrated by Sol Cotti

For my family, who taught me the power of prayer
and what it means to have faith and courage.

For Elmo, my sweet, loyal boy and coauthor.
I carry you in my heart forever.

For Petunia, thank you for mending my heart
and teaching me how to play and laugh more.

You're Surrounded By Prayers

You probably didn't know this, but at several points in your life, others have silently prayed for you. Some have sent you good vibes. Even angels disguised as humans or animals have stepped in to make you smile or heal you in passing.
Don't forget to pay it forward by praying for someone else, too.

Table of Contents

My Little Prayer Book

How To Use This Book

Within the pages of this book you will find **all kinds of prayers**. There are some to connect you with your **angels** and others to **ignite your inner power** and confidence. There are prayers for protection, breaking ancestral karma, travel, prosperity, career, family, love and more.

You can do a prayer a day by simply **flipping** through the **book** and seeing what **calls** to you. Another method is to ask the Universe to show you what prayer you **need**. Then, **open** the book and see where you are **guided**. You might want to close your eyes and ask, why this specific prayer, if you aren't sure. The **Universe speaks** to us. It's an **inner voice** that we can hear. In the next pages, I'll give you some **ideas** of when to **best pray** and how.

How To Pray

1. Praying is something simple. You can **pray** for **yourself** and **others**.

2. You can **pray** from **anywhere** or at any time. Simply **read** your prayer in the book in silence or **out loud**.

3. It is your practice and it's important to **follow** what feels good to your **heart**. If you need to harness the immediate power of prayer, I do encourage you to read it aloud. Our **words** are **vibrations** and can be felt in every cell in the body. You will feel an incredible energy of **peace** and **harmony** when you read **out loud**.

4. Another way to work with prayer is to **schedule** a **time** of day for it and **treat** it as a beautiful **ritual**.

5. Lighting a **candle** in the **morning** or **evening** to start and close your day with a prayer is a lovely suggestion. It can have a soothing, strengthening and enlightening effect on the body, mind and soul.

6. **Trust** that your **prayers** will be **answered**.

7. Ask for the Universe to **send** you a **particular sign** on a specific prayer. Say: **"Show me X sign if this will happen and you can hear my prayer."** For the sign, you can select anything like an animal, object or flower. For example, **"Show me a rainbow if I travel to Europe again this winter."**

Balancing Your Chakras Through Prayer

Prayer helps you **balance** your **chakras**. Words have a **vibration**. They can remove blocks from your **journey**. This is why, when people pray, **miracles** happen. The colors featured throughout some of the **prayers** in this book highlight a chakra that is being **aligned**.

What are Chakras?

Chakras are **spinning** energetic **wheels** inside our **bodies**. We have 7 main chakras. It is important to have them aligned because, when one is blocked, it can prevent you from achieving your goals.

Chart

Use the **chart** on the next page whenever you are wondering when a **prayer** in this book is working with a **specific chakra**.

7 Main Chakras Chart

Crown:
Location: Top of your head | **Color:** Purple or white.
Purpose: Connects you with the Universe to bring you
the guidance + direction you need.

Third Eye:
Location: In between your eyebrows | **Color:** Indigo
Purpose: Opens your eyes literally. Gives you clarity + helps you
tap into your intuition.

Throat:
Location: Throat | **Color:** Baby Blue
Purpose: Aligns your inner + external voices so that you can manifest.
(Remember, both need to be aligned in order to reel in your intentions.)

Heart:
Location: Heart | **Color:** Pink for self-love. Green for other kinds of love.
Purpose: Opens your heart to give + receive love freely
without expectations.

Solar Plexus:
Location: Stomach | **Color:** Yellow
Purpose: Powers up your strength, inner confidence + reminds you
of your limitless opportunities.

Sacral:
Location: Pelvis | **Color:** Orange
Purpose: Invigorates your joy, creativity + pleasure.

Root:
Location: Legs + feet | **Color:** Red
Purpose: Sparks grounding, reminds you that you are safe,
secure + your basics needs are being met.

What Prayers Do You Need Answered?

Jot down **below** anything you need a **prayer** for today and place today's date. The **Universe will read** these words and **answer you.** As you read this book, come back any time to this page and **add your prayer requests.** **You'll see the miracle of prayer happen.**

Daily Prayers

Prayer for Abundance

Dear Universe, I am ready and grateful to receive the abundance you have for me today. I promise to stay in the present moment to witness this abundance come in. I know it will arrive as a variety of gifts. Some blessings will be intentions I have set and others will be lovely surprises. I prepare to receive this abundance with love. I envision green light opening, cleansing and expanding my heart chakra to receive my abundance today with love and worthiness. *Namaste.*

My mantra is:
I am grounded in abundance.

Abundance is Everywhere

I **press** my dreams into ink.
I **flip** my palms up to the present moment.
I **open** my heart to receive the love.
I **smile** because I have so much to be grateful for.
Abundance is everywhere.
It's in the **sunshine**, it's in the **rain**.
It's in a **song** and in a **family gathering**.
It's in a friend's **phone call** and in a fresh bouquet of **flowers**.
It's in new **opportunities** and the **future**.
Abundance is in me.

Prayer for Balance

Dear Universe, I ask you to balance my masculine and feminine energies today. I want to know what it feels like to be soft and flow while being strong and fearless. I know having both sides of me beautifully aligned will bring great peace and success to my soul. I feel the right side of my body releasing energy while purple light is healing me. I feel the left side of my body releasing all blocks and purple light cleansing me. I feel my soul whole and powerfully aligned now. *Namaste.*

My mantra is:
I am balanced in peace.

Annie Vazquez

How to Become Balanced

I **plant** my feet on the earth.
I **place** one hand on my heart.
I **keep** the other on my belly.
I **breathe** in the sky
and **exhale** out stars.

Prayer for Calm

Dear Universe, I ask you to release me from my worry now and settle my mind, body and spirit with calm. I feel you lifting heavy burden energy off me. I feel a calmness in my head entering. I sense my shoulders relaxing. There's a gentleness in between my eyebrows. My jaw is unclenching. There is so much lightness in my heart. My stomach is tranquil. My hips feel flexible. There is sweet grounding light trickling into my legs and feet. I am in stillness now. *Namaste.*

My mantra is:
Everything is working out for me.

Everything is Working Out

Calm is **listening** to ocean waves.
It is **watching** the sunrise and
and **feeling** golden rays warmly kissing my face.
Calm is **lighting** a candle and reciting a prayer.
It is **letting go** of yesterday and tomorrow
to be here in the now.
Calm is **trusting** that everything is working out for me.

Prayer for Clarity

Dear Universe, enlighten me from my conflicted mind, body and spirit. Give me clarity and help me resolve this matter with divine wisdom. I begin to feel my tension melting away. My chest is relaxing and I am letting out a deep sigh of relief. I envision the color baby blue in between my eyebrows where my third eye is cleansing me. I feel the blocks that prevented me from seeing clearly tumbling down. Peace moves throughout my body and the guidance I need comes to me now. *Amen.*

My mantra is:
Everything is crystal clear.

The Shade of Clarity

Indigo blue is the color of the **sky** sometimes.
It is the hue of exotic **oceans**
and the vibration of my **third-eye** opening,
bringing me **clarity**.

Prayer for Good Luck

Dear Universe, please instill in me the energy of luck. I desire to know what it feels like to have luck in my life. I want to be my own lucky charm and trust that life flows in my favor. I feel the power of fortune instilled in me. It grounds my root chakra first in waves of crimson. I feel stable, safe and all my needs met. Next, it moves to my throat chakra. I feel baby blue light aligning my thoughts, words and actions. I am so lucky. *Amen.*

My mantra is:
I am my own lucky charm.

Lucky Charms

Luck is a **ladybug** crawling on my arm,
a found **penny** on the ground,
a **horseshoe** diamond necklace,
a **four-leaf clover** waving hello in a garden.
Luck is the awe from seeing a **double rainbow**
stretching its arms after the rain.
It's a winning **lottery ticket**,
and more importantly,
it's the gift of my **life**.

Prayer for Money

Dear Universe, thank you for opening up many streams of income that flow easily to me. I am ready and grateful to receive prosperity. I ask you to send red healing light to my root chakra and remove any limiting beliefs or energy blocks I have with earning money. I feel this red loving light on the top of my legs. It cascades down delicately to my knees, helping me become more flexible about receiving wealth. It trickles gently to the top and bottom of my feet. I feel grounded, stable, worthy and safe to accept money from all streams that the Universe opens to me. *Amen.*

My mantra is:
Money flows easily to me.

Money Flows Easily

Money **plants** and water **fountains**,
spotless **floors** and clean **sheets**.
A bowl of **oranges** sits and stares at the
lavender oil diffusing and dancing in the air.
With a framed photo of **Lakshmi** rising from a **lotus** flower
and a cascade of golden **coins** pouring out,
I reach my hands to **receive**. That's how
easily money flows to me when I **believe**.

Prayer for Motivation

Dear Universe, thank you for the motivation today. I am grateful to have this vibrance in me. I am ready to show up for myself. I feel passionate and driven to accomplish. This new inspiration helps me attain my goals today. I focus on all I have achieved so far. This remembrance ignites me even more. I say to myself, *I am brilliant, I am capable and I seize the day. Amen.*

My mantra is:
I am passionate, motivated and I seize the day.

Passion

I **reflect** and **remember**
my **small** and **big** achievements.
It **fuels** me to focus on how I am
brilliant, capable and **ready** to
seize the day.

Prayer for a Safe Space

Dear Universe, thank you for helping me create a safe space. I ask you to channel angelic frequency into my space and lift any low-vibrating energies that may be lingering here. Please instill what it feels like to have peace, celebration, love, good health, prosperity and harmony in this space now. I vow to do my part and honor it in many ways. I will keep it clean, tidy, smelling lovely and beautiful. I mindfully speak words of affirmation into it, like "My space is beautiful. It brings me prosperity and love." *Namaste.*

My mantra is:
My space is a reflection of me
and I give it all the TLC.

Sacred Space

Sacred space is created by
your **hands** and **voice**
in every room you enter.
Speak **words** of affirmation
into it.
Touch every nook with
love.

Prayer for House Protection

Dear Universe, thank you for protecting my home. I am grateful to have my space wrapped in your golden safeguarding light. All my loved ones and I are shielded here. My refuge is a place of harmony and abundance. As I walk around, I can feel the sacredness in the rooms, the walls, the floor and even the furniture. My plants and flowers bloom. I dream and rest so sweetly. My thoughts are clear and anchored. I feel a strong connection with my angels and ancestors here. Everything feels so good. I feel invigorated when I wake up and optimistic for a new day.
Namaste.

My mantra is:
My space is wrapped in golden safeguarding light.

Annie Vazquez

Home

My **refuge** is a place of
harmony and **abundance**.
Golden light wraps my **home**,
shielding it and
peace blooms.

Power Prayers

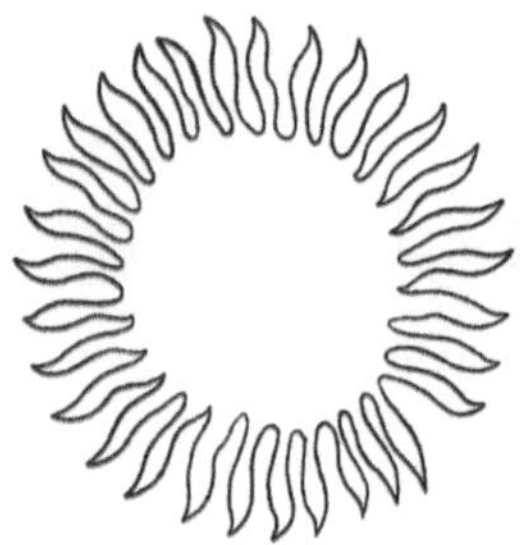

Prayer to Call Back My Power

Dear Universe, I ask you to help me call back my power today from anyone or anything that took it from me. I feel the energy pieces I left behind now being pulled back into my beautiful auric field. I sense the top of my head where my crown chakra lives regaining strength. I feel the space in between my eyebrows where my third eye exists buzzing with intuition. My throat is now relaxing and softening to speak my truth with confidence and love. My heart feels waves of harmonious love rushing in. My belly softens as soothing vibrations of strength, courage and self-confidence drop in. Gorgeous brilliant flow is swirling through my sacral chakra now and reigniting my creativity, sensuality and magnetism. My root chakra is flooded with sweet delicious grounding energy on my legs, knees and feet. Amen.

My mantra is:
I am empowered.

In My Power

In my power, I am
full of life like a seashell holding the music of the sea.
Luminous like lighting zig-zagging through the sky.
A hundred **lotus flowers** emerging from muddy water.

In my power, I am
balanced like a palm tree swaying with the wind.
Grounded like the earth bursting with golden sunflowers.
Full of light like the moon shining in the dark.

In my power I am
unlimited,
authentic,
brimming with **brilliance** and
capable of making my dreams come true.

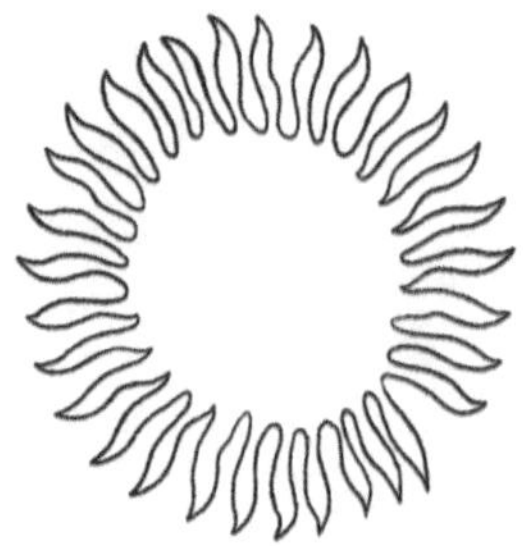

Prayer for Divine Guidance

Dear Universe, I ask you for guidance today. I ask you to communicate with me and show me what I need to do now regarding my current concern. I commit to surrendering and allowing you to illuminate me with this situation. I open myself to receiving your divine wisdom. I feel white light now sprinkling down the top of my head. It feels like beautiful soft waves on my crown chakra. I feel the downloads of your divine guidance coming in. I am ready to receive the signs, synchronization of events, music and totems you send me to help. *Namaste.*

My mantra is:
I am divinely guided.

Divine Communication

When I ask for **divine guidance**,
angel numbers appear on buildings and clocks.
When I ask for divine guidance,
totems trickle in through the repetition of animals.
When I ask for divine guidance,
synchronicity bolts in like electricity,
reeling in people, moments and messages.
All I have to do is ask to receive.

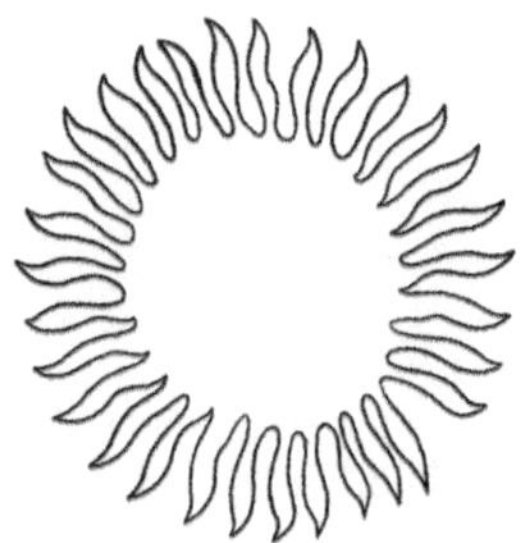

Prayer for Dreaming Bigger

Dear Universe, I want to dream bigger. I desire for my crown chakra to open up and receive downloads on what direction I should move in. Please instill in me how to dream bigger and show me what I am capable of achieving. I welcome purple healing light into my crown chakra. I feel it bringing divine wisdom to assist me. I feel my mind expanding with endless possibilities. I feel clear on my path now. *Amen.*

My mantra is:
I dream bigger today.

Opening a New Path

I open **new paths** every time
I close my eyes at night.
Worlds beyond my **imagination** appear.
Angels and **ancestors** hold my hands
and tell me to **dream** bigger.
They show me **future** glimpses of
myself and what I can **manifest** when
I choose to dream **big.**

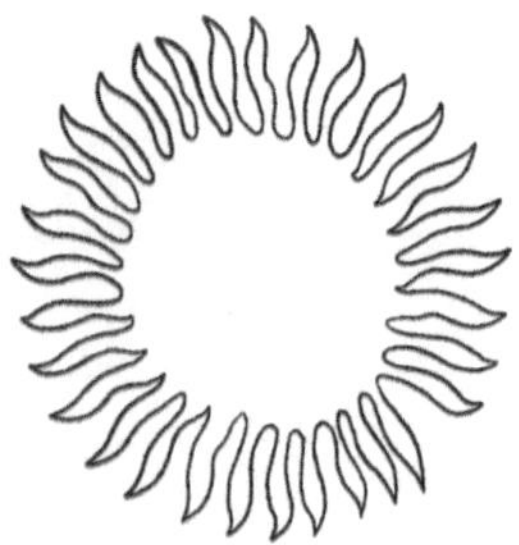

Prayer to Break Etheric Cords

Dear Universe, I ask you to grant me the fortitude to release an energy cord of attachment I formed with someone. I wish to sever this etheric cord because it is not healthy for me to psychically feel them in my spirit and take on their energy. I know breaking this cord means they can no longer drain me of my life force. I can decide to have this person in my life afterwards with a new healthy boundary. I may also choose not to have them in my life. That choice is contingent on what is in the best interest of my mental health. Please give me the sight to know what's best. To break the cord, I say their name and the following: *I now sever our cord of attachment and allow the Universe to heal us both in light.* I envision this being pulled apart. I see scissors snipping it and the rope falling. I feel instant peace and an overflowing amount of energy coming back to me. I see white healing light wrapped around my body and that person's body. Peace is now instilled. Thank you, Universe, for releasing me from this etheric cord. *Amen.*

My mantra is:
I release cords of attachment.

Life Force

In Chinese culture, *chi* means your **life force**.
It's also spelled *Qi*.
This is where your moon and sun find **balance**.
Equilibrium means **good karma**, too.
This why etheric cords need to
be broken.

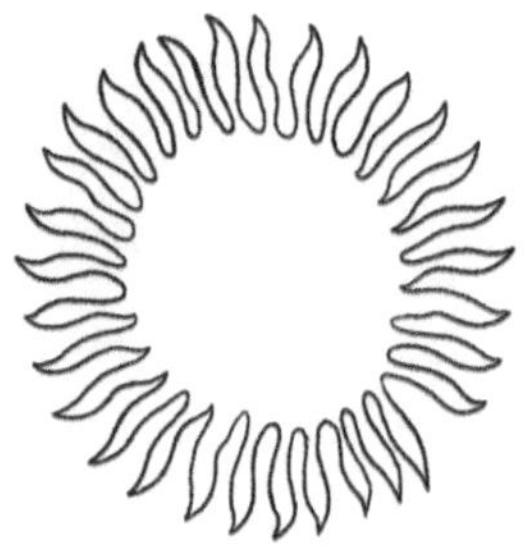

Prayer for Forgiveness

Dear Universe, give me the courage to forgive. Enlighten my heavy mind and heart. Help me release grief and anger from my body. I want to experience freedom again in forgiveness. I know forgiveness is for me and it opens new doors for the type of abundance I want to reel in. My soul deserves to be experiencing a state of bliss, love and compassion. I feel green light healing and liberating my heart. I feel purple wisdom energy cleaning and elevating my mind. *Amen.*

My mantra is:
I feel forgiveness freeing me now.

Annie Vazquez

Flowers of Forgiveness

I **open** my heart like a door
and **allow** myself to be **free**
through the flowers of **forgiveness**
that **bloom** in me.

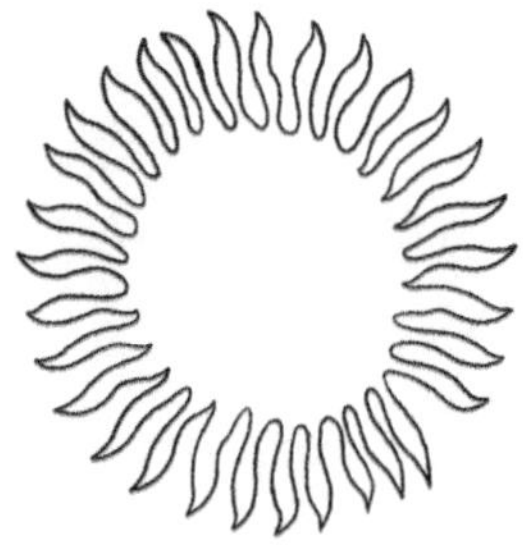

Prayer for Good Friends

Dear Universe, thank you for putting good friends in my life. I am honored to have loving, loyal, kind and supportive friendships. These special people are easy to talk to, authentic and dependable. My friends and I carve out quality time to do fun and meaningful activities. They are always there to listen, offer good advice and make me laugh. They treat me like family as I do them. I am grateful to have these amazing people in my life. I put effort in my friendships and my friends do the same. We take turns checking in, inviting each other out and showing up for one another. This creates good karma for all of us. *Namaste.*

My mantra is:
My friends are my mirrors,
reflecting light back to me.

Good Friends

When I learned to be my **own** best **friend**,
I made many **best friends**.
When I learned to **listen** to myself without judgment,
I found friends who heard me with **kind ears**.
The **tender** words I spoke to myself brought me
friends whose lips spoke with **sweet honesty** and **love**.
When I began to **show up** for myself and **value** my time,
I attracted friends who **cherished** spending time with me
and respected my **boundaries**.
My friends are my mirrors **reflecting light** back to me.

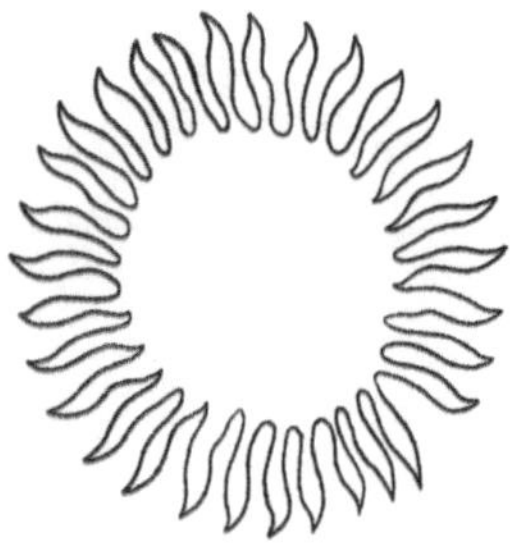

Prayer for a Miracle

Dear Universe, thank you for bringing me a miracle now with my current situation. I am so grateful for this blessing of resolve. I feel celestial energy entering in me. Purple and blue light swirl together into my crown and third eye. As I stand here in this tranquility, I feel the shift of timelines and vortexes where miracles happen, unfolding like a lotus flower. I claim my miracle now and leave the rest of how and when it will manifest up to you, Universe. *Amen.*

My mantra is:
Miracle moments manifest for me.

Miracle Moments

A **miracle** is finding something
you thought was lost.
It's **witnessing** the results
you've spent countless days and nights
working for.
The **sign** that arrives when you've
prayed for **guidance**.
It's the **wishes** you spoke into the
sky **manifesting**.

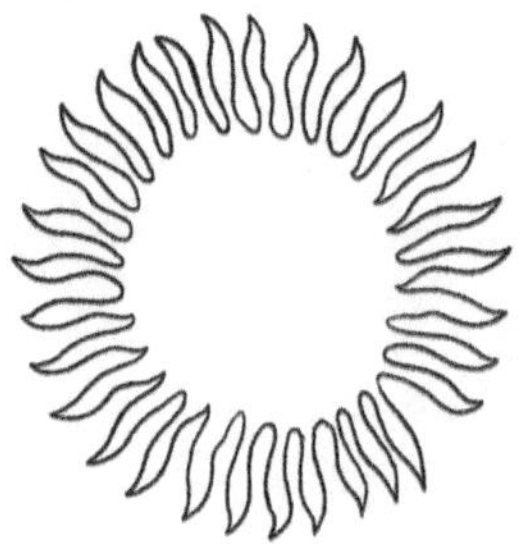

Prayer for New Doors

Dear Universe, I am ready and willing to walk through new doors. It's time for me to let go of the old me and leave the past behind. I courageously close past doors now that lead me nowhere. I ask you to enlighten me with anything else I need to do in order to step into a new me. I know and accept that when one door closes, 10 more fling open for me that will lead me to a brighter future. Thank you, Universe. *Amen.*

My mantra is:
I close old doors to open new ones.

Keys to a New Door

The universe hands me a **key** to
a **new door**
every time I **let go** of
the **past,**
pain,
people,
places,
things
and **beliefs**
that **limit** me.

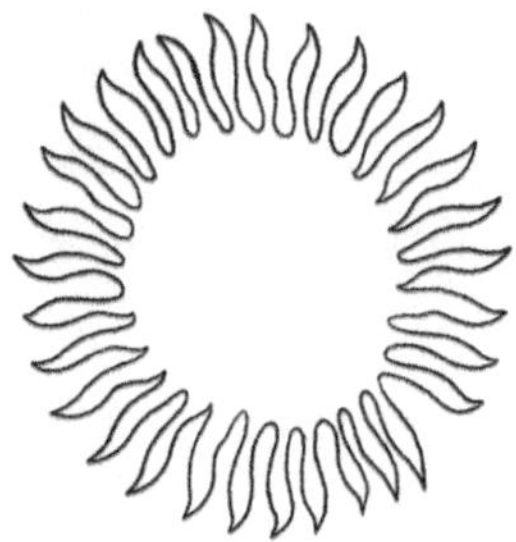

Prayer to Release Blocks

Dear Universe, I am ready now to tear down my blocks and release them from my mind, body and spirit. I am ready to do the work to climb the mountain I wish to stand on. I desire to be united with my intentions. I ask you to balance all my chakras now in this prayer so I can begin the process. I feel purple light in my crown. I feel indigo light in my third eye. I feel baby blue light in my throat. I feel green light in my heart. I feel yellow light in my stomach. I feel orange light in my pelvis. I feel red light in my legs and feet. These healing colors mesh and make a rainbow inside me. *Namaste.*

My mantra is:
I am balanced and block free.

Burning Blocks Letter

What **feels** heavy within,
I **pull** out of me and let it **pour**
onto sheets of **paper**.
Pain, anger, fears, old **memories**
stare back from line to **line**,
wanting to crawl back into **me**, but
I **strike** a match.
Their ashes **rise** with the wind.
My **glorious** new chapter is about to **begin**.

Good Health Prayers

Prayer for Good Sleep

Dear Universe, thank you for good sleep. I am grateful for rest and rejuvenation. I let go of what happened earlier and what has to happen next. I surrender knowing that you are handling everything for me and it's all working out in my favor. I know that when I wake up from this healing slumber, I will receive guidance and good news. I will look gorgeous and feel wonderful. I am excited to have sweet delicious dreams. I invite my divine team to visit me with messages and my body to detox. *Amen.*

My mantra is:
I sleep deeply and sweetly.

Sweet Dreams

Sweet **dreams** start with
a warm bath, **washing** away
the **day**,
slipping into cozy pajamas,
sipping on a cup of warm
chamomile tea,
before **tucking** myself into
bed with soft **perfumed**
lavender sheets and pillows
and **surrendering** into slumber.

Prayer for Healthy Pregnancy

Dear Universe, I ask you to bless me with a healthy pregnancy. I feel orange light coming into my sacral chakra now. It aligns me and removes any toxic energy or limiting karmic beliefs. If I made any vows in a past life to not have kids, I release those vows. Universe, instill in me your definition of fertility now so I can welcome the angelic realm to be with me and my future baby. I relinquish control and allow our Guardian Angels to lead us through this easy, happy and healthy pregnancy where my baby and I are safe and excited to be together this lifetime. *Amen.*

My mantra is:
I have a healthy pregnancy

To Be a Mother

To be a **mother** is a role
I wish for my **soul**.

It is a **cosmic** journey
I am ready to take
my **body**, **mind** and **spirit** on.

It is a **dream**
to carry **sacred** life in my **womb**
and see my **belly bloom**.

I am **yin**,
I am **moon**,
I am **portal**,
I am **mother**.

Prayer for Mental Healing

Dear Universe, help me heal my mind today. I ask you to send angelic white light and purple divine wisdom to my crown chakra. I place my hands on my head now to feel the healing light gently curing me. I feel it lifting off low vibrating energy. It clears my mind, bringing me harmony. My energy transforms from caterpillar to butterfly, thriving in peace and trust. Thank you for sending me this beautiful potent energy. *Amen.*

My mantra is:
My mind is filled with harmony.

Gateway to the Universe

My **crown** chakra is the gateway to
the **Universe**.
I become **whole** again
like a Full **Moon**
every time I ask for **healing**.

Prayer for Optimal Health

Dear Universe, thank you for my optimal health. It is a wonderful feeling to know that my entire body is in shape and operating perfectly for my age. I am a healthy weight and I can move with ease. My mind is aligned, clear and optimistic. My bones are powerful. My muscles are fit. My joints are strong. My organs work beautifully. I am so grateful to constantly be getting healthier and healthier every day. *Amen.*

My mantra is:
My body, mind and spirit are healthy.

Healthy Feels Like

Healthy **feels** like waking up
with a **smile** on your face as
you **open** the window shades
to **unveil** a fresh new day of
endless **possibilities** rising
like a **sunrise**.

Prayer for Physical Healing

Dear Universe, thank you for healing my body. I place my hands on the part of my body where I need it the most. I feel angelic white light pouring into me like medicine. It alleviates my pain and aches, and begins to cure me. I feel my physical body becoming lighter, stronger and healthier. I continue to repeat this prayer every day until I am fully healed. *Amen.*

My mantra is:
My body is a temple of good health.

Healing with Angels

Angelic light **enters** me from
the **heavens**.
When I **pray** for
my body to be **healed**,
it pours into me like **medicine**.

Prayer for a Successful Surgery

Dear Universe, thank you for a successful surgery. I am so grateful to have an incredible doctor who is seasoned, passionate and creates triumphant results for their patients. I trust my doctor. They demonstrate to me they care for my health and well-being. I feel safe and cared for. I know that my angels, ancestors and divine team have guided me to this doctor and will also be with me during the procedure. They will watch over me and keep me healthy. After my procedure, my body will heal and operate better than ever. *Amen.*

My mantra is:
My surgery is successful
and goes better than I expected.

Divine Healing

When I ask the Universe for **healing**,
I am divinely **guided** to many
healers who **care** for my well-being
and know how to **help** me.

Prayer for Weight Loss

Dear Universe, thank you for helping me get healthier. My body feels so good letting go of extra baggage. What a glorious release to feel lighter and stronger in my body. I am blessed to have healed the root of why I gained excess weight so it never comes back on. I am committed to this lifestyle change. I will eat healthier portion sizes, exercise and practice mindfulness because I love all of me. I honor my body by speaking kind and encouraging words to it. All of this amplifies my self-love. *Amen.*

My mantra is:
I love and treasure myself.

Love Myself

I tell myself, *I love you,* and
sadness and anger leave out
the **door** of my **heart**.
I tell myself, *I love you,* and
a field of lavender blooms
calmness in my veins.
I love me, I love me, I love me
is the the most **beautiful song** to
sing to **myself** every morning.
I tell myself, *I love you,*
and a sun **rises** with **courage**
in my belly.

Family Prayers

Prayer for Family Healing

Dear Universe, please send your comforting, healing light and love energy to my family. I ask you to give us all strength and courage to heal at this moment. Let this healing be felt by our ancestors and our future generations. I feel a string of white celestial light going into me and my family's hearts now. I see it slowly and softly swirling in and removing pain that doesn't serve our greatest and highest selves. I sense giant waves of energy being lifted off us. So much relief is felt. *Amen.*

My mantra is:
My family is majestically healed.

My Beautiful Family Tree

I am the **seed** of my ancestors.
Within my **blood** are the stories of their souls,
ancient **wisdom**
I **carry** wherever I go.

I am a seed of my **ancestors**.
A beating **heart**, a courageous **light**.
A spirit who doesn't give up the **fight**.

I am the seed of my ancestors,
and I water my **family tree** by
praying, meditating and **loving** naturally.

Prayer for Releasing Ancestral Karma

Dear Universe, I ask you to help me release ancestral karma. I am ready to shed this trauma that runs in my veins. I wish to be free and only inherit the joy, courage, determination and unconditional love my ancestors experienced. I can feel you lifting and releasing my mind and heart from their old wounds. I feel myself, my present family and my ancestors being healed simultaneously. I feel harmony instilled in all generations now.
Namaste.

My mantra is:
I inherit good family karma.

Good Family Karma

Good family **karma** is self-love.
It's compassionate **communication**.
It's **standing up** for oneself and
igniting **faith** when things get tough.
It's a flood of **prosperity** that
can be used to **help** the world.
It's feeling worthy to be **authentic** and
taking **care** of yourself first so you can
cultivate good family karma.

Prayer for My Inner Child

Dear Universe, thank you for helping me heal my inner child. I call back any fragmented pieces my little soul may have left behind in painful situations. I ask you to purify these pieces. I feel you pouring white healing energy over these pieces, repairing them and melding them back to my spirit. My mind, body and spirit are fully restored. I feel whole again at this moment. I promise to nurture and give my inner child what it needs. Whether it is to pursue a goal, play or laugh and enjoy life more. *Amen.*

My mantra is:
I nurture and nourish my inner child.

Little Me Lives

Little me **lives** in my adult
body.
I cradle that **child** in the safeness
of my arms and **whisper** to her
the **words** she needed to hear.
I **remind** her not to give up because
her **dreams** are still **possible**.
I tell her she is **beautiful** and unique,
she is **talented** and worthy, and
I show **her** how to laugh and play **again**.

Prayer for My Father

Dear Universe, thank you for my father. Today, I honor him for all the sacrifices he's made to help me lead a wonderful life. Bless my father for his heart of gold and for choosing to raise me the best way he could with unconditional love, kindness and good morals. I thank him for all he did to put a roof over my head, food on the table, get me to school and all the extra gifts he gave me. I celebrate him for always being there to guide and support me. How lucky I am to know a beautiful soul like my dad who loves me for me. *Amen.*

My mantra is:
I honor my divine father.

Divine Father

A **divine** father
offers his **unconditional** love
from his **gentle** fearless heart.
He cradles and **shields** you.
He is your **guiding** light in a world where
one must learn to be **soft** and **strong**.
Divine father pours **inspiration** into your cup
so you never go thirsty
while creating your **dreams**.

Prayer for My Mother

Dear Universe, thank you for my mother. Today, I honor her for all the sacrifices she's made to help me lead a wonderful life. Bless my mother for her heart of gold and for choosing to raise me the best way she could, with unconditional love, kindness and good morals. I thank her for all she did to put a roof over my head, food on the table, get me to school and all the extra gifts she gave me. I celebrate her for always being there to guide and support me. How lucky I am to know a beautiful soul like my mom who loves me for me. *Amen.*

My mantra is:
I honor my divine mother.

Divine Mother

A **divine** mother
shares **unconditional**
love with you.
Her's is the first **heart-**
beat you hear from
the **womb**,
a drumming **song**
your ears will always **remember**.

Prayer for My Son

Dear Universe, thank you for my son. I am grateful for my beautiful child. What a blessing to call him family. Today, I ask you to strengthen his faith and encourage him to believe that dreams are possible. Remind him storms are temporary, just like rainbows. Give him patience and compassion to be in the present moment. Allow him to understand all we have is now. Guide him to achieve good health, happiness and success. *Amen.*

My mantra is:
The Universe blesses my son.

Remind Your Sons

Remind your **sons** they
are **loved**.
Teach them to be
like trees,
standing tall, able
to **weather** the worst
and still **bloom**,
season after season.

Prayer for My Daughter

Dear Universe, thank you for my daughter. I am grateful for my beautiful child. What a blessing to call her family. Today, I ask you to strengthen her faith and encourage her to believe that dreams are possible. Remind her storms are temporary, just like rainbows. Give her patience and compassion to be in the present moment. Guide her to achieve good health, happiness and success. *Amen.*

My mantra is:
The Universe blesses my daughter.

Daughter

You are a **field**
of white **roses**
blossoming in my **heart.**

Prayer for My Grandfather

Dear Universe, thank you for my grandfather. I am grateful for him. He is the definition of unwavering love. I admire him so much and all he does for me and my family. My grandfather is a wise soul who teaches me so much. I am a better person because of him and he holds a special place in my heart. Today, I ask you to bless my grandfather with good health, joy and protection. May he always know how much he means to me.
Namaste.

My mantra is:
The Universe blesses my grandfather.

Grandfather

A grandfather's **love** is so **powerful**.
It **will** always have a
special place in your *corazon* or **heart**.

Prayer for My Grandmother

Dear Universe, thank you for my grandmother. I am grateful for her. She is the definition of unwavering love. I admire her so much and all she does for me and my family. My grandmother is a wise soul who teaches me so much. I am a better person because of her and she holds a special place in my heart. Today, I ask you to bless my grandmother with good health, joy and protection. May she always know how much she means to me.
Namaste.

My mantra is:
The Universe blesses my beautiful grandmother.

Grandmother

A grandmother's love is the **sweetest**
amor or **love**
to have **ever** existed.

Prayer for My Grandson

Dear Universe, thank you for my grandson. I am grateful for him. He is one of my greatest gifts in this lifetime. What an honor to call him family. Today, I ask you to light his path. Keep my dear grandson wrapped in a golden light of protection. Guide him as he journeys through mountains and valleys. Let his head stay casted up at the brilliance of the stars rather than looking down in fear. Please illuminate my mind and heart on how to be the grandparent he needs. Bless his heart, dreams and life. *Amen.*

My mantra is:
The Universe blesses my grandson.

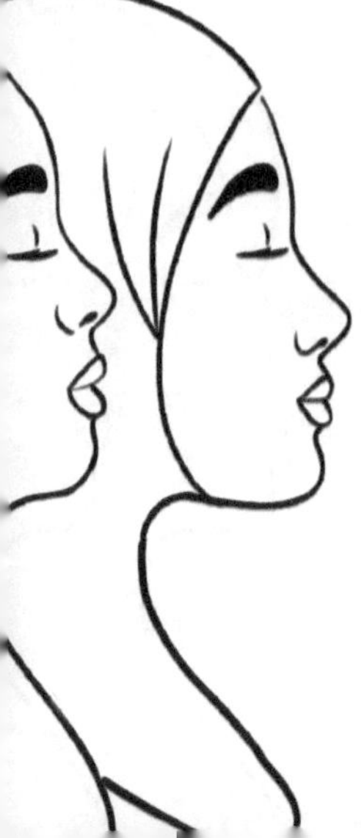

Grandson

May your **head** stay
casted up, **gazing** at
the brilliance of the **stars** so
you remember **you** are one, too.

Prayer for My Granddaughter

Dear Universe, thank you for my granddaughter. I am grateful for her. She is one of my greatest gifts in this lifetime. What an honor to call her family. Today, I ask you to light her path. Keep my dear granddaughter wrapped in a golden light of protection. Guide her as she journeys through mountains and valleys. Let her head stay casted up at the brilliance of the stars rather than looking down in fear. Please illuminate my mind and heart on how to be the grandparent she needs. Bless her heart, dreams and life.
Amen.

My mantra is:
The Universe blesses my granddaughter.

Granddaughter

You are
the **glowing** candle
of my **prayers**.

Prayer for My Uncle

Dear Universe, thank you for my uncle and role model. I am grateful for him. What an honor to call him family. Today, I ask you to keep my dear uncle filled with joy, faith and protection. Illuminate his mind, body and spirit to the path of his greatest happiness. Always remind him what a difference he has made in my life and how much I cherish him.
Amen.

My mantra is:
The Universe blesses my uncle.

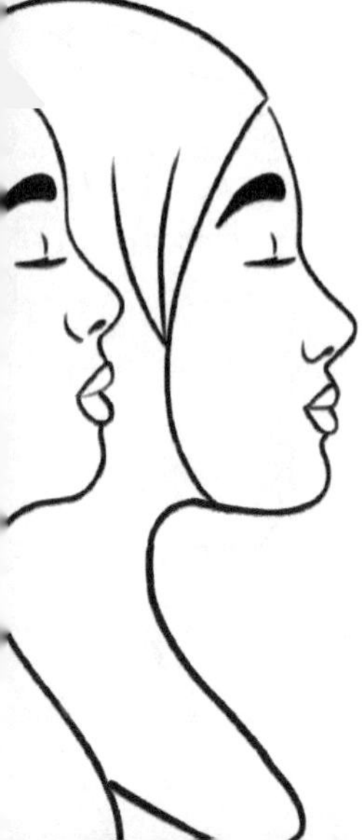

95

Uncle

You are a **strong** mountain
and a **courageous** sunrise
that always **finds** a way
to climb the sky
and share your **light**.

Prayer for My Aunt

Dear Universe, thank you for my aunt and role model. I am grateful for her. What an honor to call her family. Today, I ask you to keep my dear aunt filled with joy, faith and protection. Illuminate her mind, body and spirit to the path of her greatest happiness. Always remind her how much she means to me; her smile, softness and loving heart. *Amen.*

My mantra is:
The Universe blesses my aunt.

Aunt

You are my **shooting star**,
forever reminding me
to let my **dreams**
lead me.

Prayer for My Nephew

Dear Universe, thank you for my nephew. I am grateful for him. What an honor to call him family. Today, I ask you to light his path. Keep my dear nephew wrapped in a golden light of protection. Guide him as he journeys through mountains and valleys. Let his head stay casted up at the brilliance of the stars rather than looking down in fear. Please illuminate my mind and heart on how to be the aunt/uncle he needs. Bless his heart, dreams and life. *Amen.*

My mantra is:
The Universe blesses my nephew.

Nephew

Our **family** needed
another **angel** and
the Universe **created**
you.

Prayer for My Niece

Dear Universe, thank you for my niece. I am grateful for her. What an honor to call her family. Today, I ask you to light her path. Keep my dear niece wrapped in a golden light of protection. Guide her as she journeys through mountains and valleys. Let her head stay casted up at the brilliance of the stars rather than looking down in fear. Please illuminate my mind and heart on how to be the aunt/uncle she needs. Bless her heart, dreams and life. *Amen.*

My mantra is:
The Universe blesses my niece.

Niece

The **day** you were born,
my heart **bloomed**
a thousand **sunflowers**.

Prayer for My Pet

Dear Universe, thank you for the perfect best friend. I am so grateful to have this little angel you gifted me. Bless my little soulmate. Guide me so that they always feel safe, understood and comforted at all times. Show me how to make their life extra special and joyous. Help me communicate with them so that we can understand each other easily. Please, protect them and keep my precious angel happy and healthy. *Namaste.*

My mantra is:
My pet is happy and healthy.

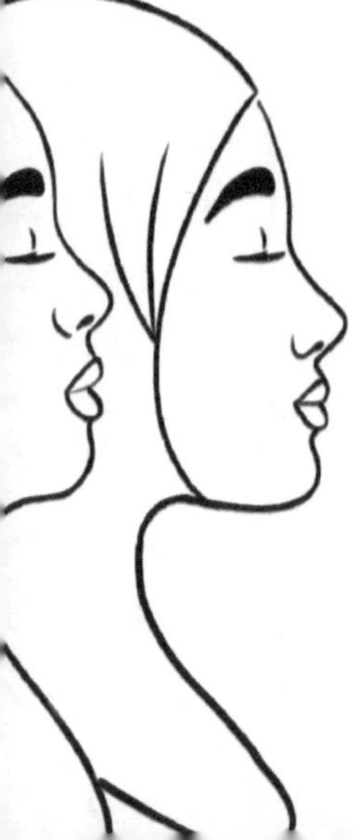

Little Best Friend

Wet **kisses,**
soft little **snores.**
Blissful **barks,**
gentle **purrs.**
My furry little **best friend** is
all I ever **wanted** and more.

Prayers for Healing Relationships

Prayer for Closure

Dear Universe, thank you for helping me achieve closure. It feels good to have peace now with this matter. I know I did the best I could in this situation. I placed so much effort and time into it, but now, I leave it in your hands. Universe, I surrender, let go and close the book on this concern. I trust you will know exactly what to do with it. I ask you to instill in me strength to stay moving forward and not look back, second-guessing my decision. Please send healing light to me and any parties involved. *Amen.*

My mantra is:
I have peace and closure.

Closing a Book

Sometimes, it's hard to **walk** away, but
then the Universe **whispers,**
it's the only way, so
I **surrender**, let go and **close** the book,
trusting in tomorrow.

Prayer for a Peaceful Divorce

Dear Universe, thank you for helping me achieve a peaceful divorce. I learned a lot of lessons in this relationship. It helped my soul grow exponentially, but I am now ready to release this sacred union and move forward. I wish my former partner love and light. I am grateful that both of us can part ways amicably. It is a wonderful feeling to witness all the legalities in this matter flow positively and reach closure. As we both move into the future on different journeys, I ask you to continue to help us heal our hearts, minds and bless both of our new paths. *Amen.*

My mantra is:
My divorce is peaceful.

A Final Chapter

A final chapter in **love** ends with
a **sacred** union coming apart to give
two souls **new** opportunities
on different **journeys**.
Endings are also **beginnings**.

Prayer for Loss

Dear Universe, I would like you to help me heal from this loss. I feel a void and deep pain from this experience. I ask you to ease my suffering so I can get through this. I feel green light enveloping my heart at this moment and helping me release the heavy emotions I am carrying. I take a deep breath in and allow the Universe to relax my mind, take away my negative thoughts and convert them to optimistic ones. I take another breath in and feel my courage rising like the sun in my belly. It reminds me I will smile again and get through this challenging period. *Namaste.*

My mantra is:
I peacefully accept the things I cannot control.

The Light of Hope

Courage rises in my belly like the sun
and I am **reminded** that, even when
I **feel** like I'm in the dark,
there is always a light of **hope**
to **guide** me out.

Love Prayers

Prayer for Self-Love

Dear Universe, empower me with your loving light. Show me how to better love myself. Instill in me the way I can accept that I am good enough, beautiful, smart, talented, brave and worthy of self-love. Teach me to show up for myself, give it my all and follow my heart's calling. I know that I attract as I am. The more I work on myself, the more love will flow around me. I feel your healing pink light beaming into my heart, opening it up and pulling out any limiting beliefs. Thank you for instilling in me your definition of self-love. I am excited to treasure the greatest love: myself.
Namaste.

My mantra is:
I am my greatest love.

Your Greatest Love

Your greatest **love** is staring
back in the **mirror** at you.
Remind her, daily, she is
the **moon** and the **sun** so that
nobody will have the **power** to
dim her **light**.

Buy her flowers, perfume and chocolates
because she **deserves** feminine **gifts**.
Book her plane tickets and take her
around the **world**.
Give her **adventures** and **memories** to
last a **lifetime**.
Compliment her with
physical and **soulful** words so that
she'll never settle for anything less.

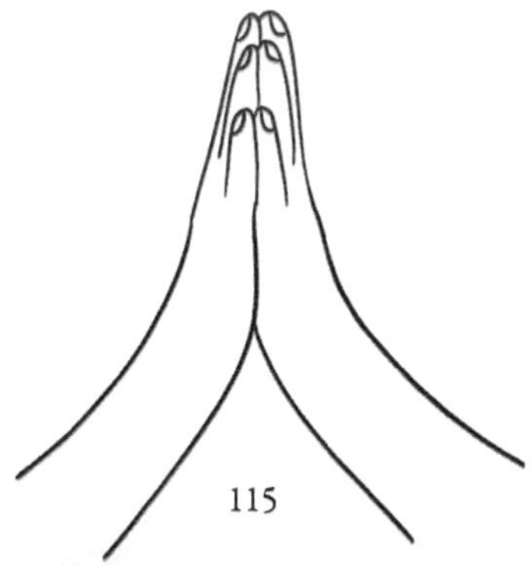

Prayer for Self-Confidence

Dear Universe, thank you for helping me feel confident. Please instill in me your definition of what confidence means in my body, mind and spirit. I want to know what it feels like to be good enough as I am. I wish to wake up every day and go after my dreams without hesitation. I want to know what it feels like to believe in myself and not be afraid to follow my heart. I feel yellow light expanding in my stomach area, soothing and recharging my solar plexus. I am fueled with inner confidence now. Yes, I am confident. Yes, I will achieve this. Yes, I got this! *Amen.*

My mantra is:
I am good enough.

Self-Confidence

Self-confidence is a **flashlight** leading
you through a dark **road**.
It's the sun **bravely** peeking out from
behind a shy cloud.
It's a **voice** that sounds like a seesaw,
going up and down until it finds its
perfect pitch.
It's the voice within that says, *I might
be afraid, but I am going to **do** it anyway.*

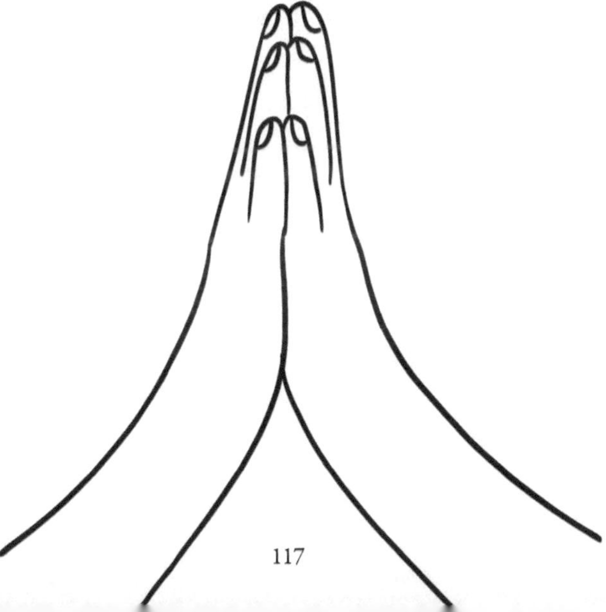

Prayer for Romantic Soulmate Love

Dear Universe, I am grateful for the deep self-love that I have for myself and all the inner work I have done to reach this point. I know that the more I treasure myself and celebrate life, I will invite in the perfect partner. I am excited to see my reflection in this beautiful person. This love is loyal, kind, sweet, thoughtful, emotionally intelligent and pure of heart. I feel a green light burning inside me now like a flame calling my partner. In divine time, they will be united with me. *Amen.*

My mantra is:
My heart is open and ready to receive.

Soulmate Love

A green light **dances** inside my **heart** chakra
like the **aurora borealis** when
I **remember** that I will be
united with my **romantic**
soulmate partner one day.

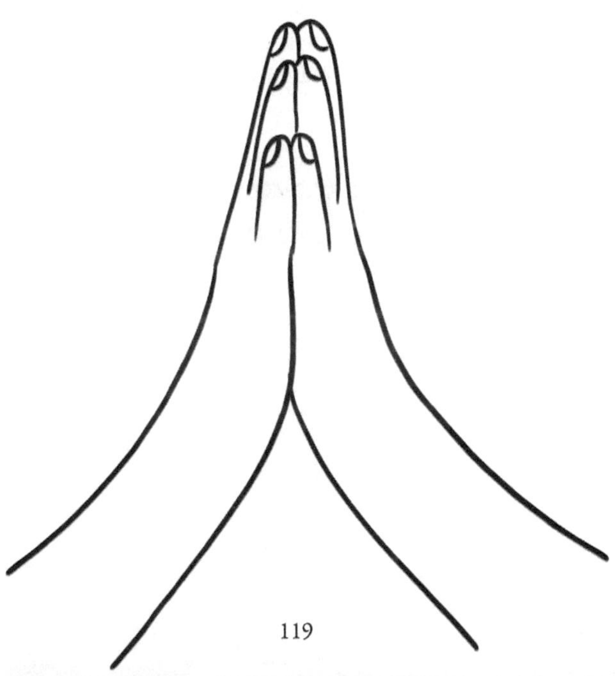

Prayer for Marriage

Dear Universe, I would like to be married and experience what a loving, committed soulmate relationship feels like in this lifetime. I ask you to bless me with this beautiful partnership. I dream of forming a forever union with someone who possesses a good heart, has emotional intelligence, is playful, fun and honest. I ask you to unite me with someone who has self-love like me and can love me deeply and unconditionally. Together, I envision us having a magnetic attraction on the soul, mental and physical realms. Please bring me someone who I can share my life with, and together, we can be beacons of light to one another and to the world. I am open to receiving healing in all my chakras now and my beautiful dream marriage. *Amen.*

My mantra is:
I am happily married.

Sweet Union

Two rings to symbolize our **union**.
Two **paths** merging so we can walk
together on one.
Two doves to represent the **peace**
we have **found** in each other.
Two lives sharing one **love**.

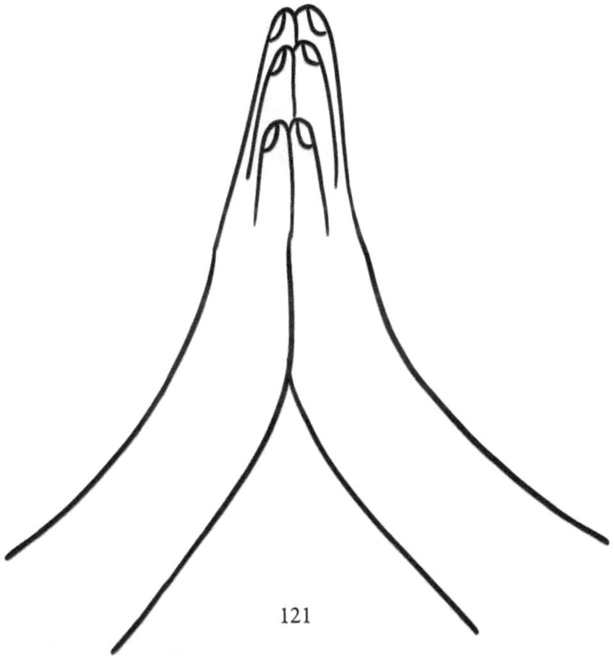

Prayer for My Wedding

Dear Universe, thank you for my beautiful wedding. Everything I have envisioned for my special sacred union manifests even more picturesque. It is a dream come true to experience this moment with the love of my life. The mood, design and backdrop is aesthetically perfect. Our looks, rings and energy exudes ideal elegance. I am so grateful to have the most caring guests present to witness our matrimony. They offer us heart-filled blessings and celebrate our love with us. I ask you, Universe, to protect my marriage and guide us during this holy ceremony and throughout the remainder of our lives. *Amen.*

My mantra is:
My wedding is the perfect sacred ceremony.

Wedding Bells

A **sacred** ritual celebrates
our souls' love in **ceremony**,
our guests' pure **blessings**.
My **love** and I loop
rings on each other,
intertwining our spirits for
a **lifetime**.

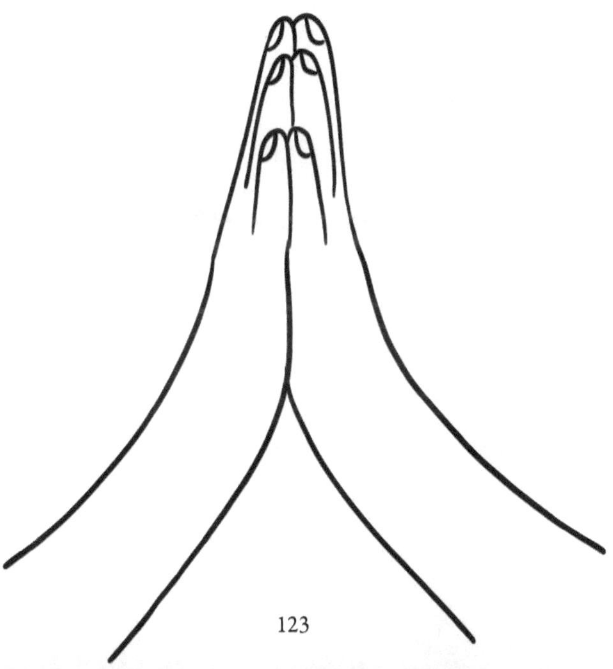

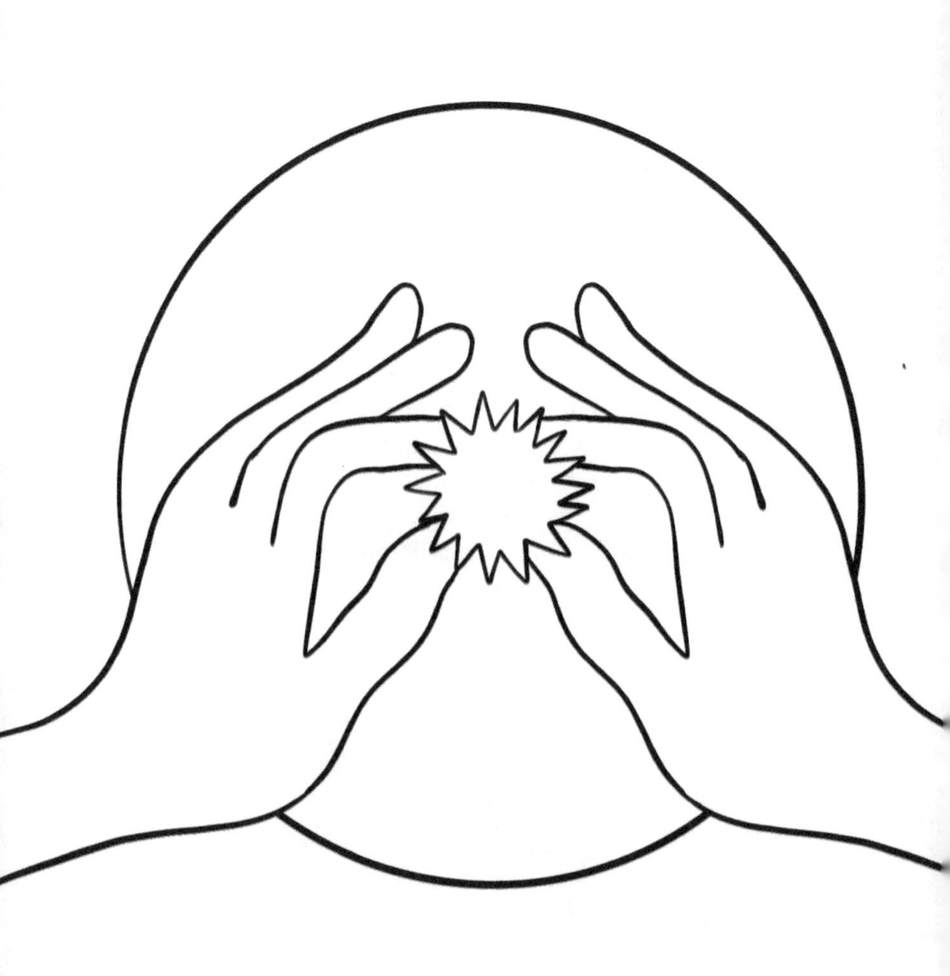

Goal Prayers

Prayer for Passing a Test

Dear Universe, thank you for helping me pass my exam. I am so grateful to get to this next point of my journey. Instill in me the courage to study and be focused for this test. I visualize myself passing my exam with calm, ease and a good score. I envision myself completing it with a big smile of success. I feel your healing power pouring illumination into me. I feel red light coming into my legs for grounding. I sense yellow light charging my solar plexus with inner confidence and courage. I see indigo blue light opening my third eye so that my intuition guides me and I trust my answers. *Amen.*

My mantra is:
I am ready to achieve and pass my test.

Success is Mine

I am ready to **pass**,
focused, calm and courageously.
It is my **birthright** to have success.
I dig into my soul's limitless **power**,
the one in my belly that **rises** like the sun,
and **remember** I am a child of the
Universe,
bright and full of **miracles**.
Success is mine.

Prayer for My Project

Dear Universe, thank you for helping me on my project. It feels good to know that this project is going to be a success. I am thrilled it surpasses my goals. I follow my intuition and heart while working on it. I pour so much love and light on it that it begins to naturally take its form. Every time I begin working on it, I thank it for existing and the wonderful purpose it will have in this world. I ask you to cleanse my sacral chakra, which is connected to my creativity. I envision orange light moving in me. I feel sparks of inspiration and passion. *Amen.*

My mantra is:
My project surpasses my goals.

Orange Light Glimmers in Me

Orange light **glimmers** in me every time
I tap into my inner child and **create**
from the heart. I **birth** projects
and incredible **possibilities** open like portals
to dimensions **flowing** with **love** and **purpose**.

Prayer for Graduation

Dear Universe, thank you for helping me graduate today. I am proud of myself. I am overjoyed to celebrate this milestone. I am grateful for sticking through hours of studying, tests and projects to achieve this moment. I commemorate my graduation by doing something meaningful to recognize the ending of one adventure to begin a new one. I honor myself with rest and relaxation so my mind, body and spirit are refreshed for this next phase of my life. *Amen.*

My mantra is:
I graduate into a new adventure.

Graduation

Hours of **studying**,
countless **exams** and projects,
a new **milestone**,
a **chapter** closed.
A new **adventure** awaits.

Prayer for Career

Dear Universe, thank you for my dream career. I love what I do to earn an income. I am paid exactly what I desire and the people I work with are appreciative and kind. My work schedule is perfect for my lifestyle, and I am passionate and excited to work my dream career every day. It lights up my heart. I have a beautiful balance in my life with my career and my "me" time. I know that my career arrives in divine timing. Everything I have done until now for work has connected the dots and led me to this moment. This is my dharma. *Amen.*

My mantra is:
I love my career.

The Road to My Dharma

My **heart** is my **compass**
It shows me the **road** to
my **dharma**.

Prayer for Moving

Dear Universe, I am excited for my move to a new home. I created a list of details to help you comprehend what kind of space I am ready to live in. I put together a vision book with images defining my aesthetic, budget and how I want it to look and feel. Universe, I know you love details so I add a copious amount to my intention. I ask for it to be safe and spacious; a home where love and celebrations take place. I surrender now to you in guiding me on the next steps. Thank you, Universe. *Amen.*

My mantra is:
I love my new home.

Home Sweet Home

A perfect **home** has walls that **hug** you
when **you** walk in and
floors that **hold** you up
whenever you've had a challenging day.
It is where windows **show** you to look out
and **dream** big, but also to look within
and **remember** to be grateful for where you
are right now because the **present** is
a **gift**.

Prayer to Sell My Home

Dear Universe, thank you for helping me sell my home. I am grateful to my house and all the lessons, growth and love it brought me. I now release this space with love and light. I cut off any cord of attachments I may have to this residence with peace. I invite in now the perfect buyer to sell this place to. This purchaser is wonderful and I receive a beautiful amount of compensation for my home. This is a speedy, easy and blessed transaction. I am excited to give the purchaser their keys and move onto my new adventure and home. *Namaste.*

My mantra is:
I sell my home with joy
and receive great prosperity for it.

Annie Vazquez

New Adventures

I **pack** my bags.
I don't **look** back,
for what I need to **remember**
I carry in my heart **forever**.

Prayer for Travel

Dear Universe, thank you for opening doors to travel. I am ready for adventures and grand new memories away from home. I create a vision book with images and details of the cities and countries I wish to visit. My vision comes to fruition. I am grateful for these safe journeys that are picturesque, heart-filling and full of good times. I love that everything manifests with flow. I pack the perfect items with calmness. I am gifted a copious travel fund, all the proper documents to travel with ease, as well as arriving and departing on time. I love my accommodations, the people I encounter and travel with and the wonderful energy I receive from my trips. *Amen.*

My mantra is:
I am a globetrotter.

Adventure Door

I open the adventure **door** to
cities and countries I **dream** of.
A **vision** book filled with details
packs my suitcase to these
picturesque places.
Click, click, click
goes my camera, **capturing**
memories to last me a **lifetime**.

Special Day Prayers

Prayer for My Birthday

Dear Universe, thank you for helping me make another trip around the sun. I am grateful to celebrate my life today and all I have. I honor the candles I place on my cake, which represent my beautiful years of life. I reflect on the moments that have led me here. I recount my small and big wins, the tears, laughter, joy and the people in my life. I write down 12 wishes for this new cycle. I light my candles, close my eyes and envision these wishes coming true before blowing them out. A year from today, I will witness my special birthday wishes manifested. *Amen.*

My mantra is:
I celebrate my life.

A Trip Around the Sun

Another **journey** complete.
Small and big **wins**:
tears,
laughter,
joy
and the **people**
in my **life**.

Gratitude.
A set of dancing **candles**
to **celebrate**
each **trip**
around the **sun**
and a full **heart** remembering
all the **fun**.

Prayer for a New Season

Dear Universe, thank you for this new season. I know each one is a stepping stone leading me to my best and highest self. I am prepared and excited for these fresh three months to co-create with you my beautiful life. I take action by writing detailed intentions of what I desire to invite in and the abundance I long to experience. I make festive changes to my space to invoke the magic of this time. I bring in seasonal plants, fruits, decor, place a motivational mantra up, work on my vision book and keep my space tidy. Lastly, I do a daily activity as simple as lighting a candle and reading a prayer to strengthen my faith. *Amen.*

My mantra is:
I expect the best this season and I am open to the glorious surprise of how it will unfold for me.

A New Season Starts

A new **season** starts with
seasonal plants and fruits **blooming**,
a **motivating** mantra hanging on a door,
cutting out and pasting new **dreams** on a
board so you never stop **envisioning**
the **future** you desire and deserve.

Prayer for a New Week

Dear Universe, as I commence this new week, I ask you to make it the best 7 days. 7 is a powerful number. It means obstacle-free and miraculous creation. I am ready for both. I tap into the energy of this number now and I claim my abundance. I commit to working with the energy of this number by practicing a healing practice at 7 a.m. and 7 p.m. for the next 7 days. Thank you, Universe, for this incredible new week. *Amen.*

My mantra is:
Every day, I am gifted with 7 beautiful gifts.

Seven

7 is a **lucky** number,
the **number** of creation.
Obstacles dissipate in this **vibration** and
I taste sweet delicious **opportunities** like honey.

Prayer for a New Month

Dear Universe, as I enter this new month, keep me protected, grounded and surrounded with celebrations. I show up for my soul, goals and dreams. I set daily small intentions with faith to get me to my bigger intentions down the line. My daily attitude and actions are positive and aligned to determine my reality. I am excited for this chapter and the glorious blissful adventures it brings me. I am ready to laugh, dance, kiss and toast daily to my beautiful life. I invite in a life rich with love, romance, prosperity, travel, healthy relationships and peace. *Amen.*

My mantra is:
This month, I shine.

Main Character

I am the main character of my **life**
and, every month,
I have a whole blank **book**
to **fill** with the way
I want my **story** to come alive.

Prayer for a New Year

Dear Universe, I ask you to guide me into this new 12-month cycle of celebration. I am ready to make it my best year. Help me follow my intuition, practice stillness and open my arms to accept and give out the best. I vow to take action by making space for my success. I clean my home, heart, and mind, and leave the past behind. I utilize my full power in the present by writing down 12 wishes of mine for the next 12 months. I go the extra mile to create a vision book dedicated to these goals with details and images. Every month, I revisit it to make tweaks or add wishes.
I slowly start to see these wishes actualize. *Amen.*

My mantra is:
My daily actions bring my dreams to fruition.

12 Wishes

12 **grapes** at midnight.
A bowl of **lentils**.
The clink of **champagne** glasses.
Fireworks exploding in the sky.

Red **underwear** to bring in love.
An all white **dress** for inner peace.
A bucket of **water** tossed into the street to
wash out what no longer serves me,
and a **prayer** to call in what does.

Lunar Cycle Prayers

Prayer for Fall Equinox

Dear Universe, thank you for this new season of harvest and magic. I am optimistic to start reaping what I have sown. I know that my ritual, mindset, detailed intentions and actions get me to my dreams. I am ready for cooler weather and shorter days of light. I am preparing for autumn. I sweep my floors with a cinnamon broom to bless my foundations with a steady flow of abundance and prosperity. I bring items that represent harvest, such as pumpkins, apples and acorns, into my home. These items amplify the energy of the season and help me manifest more harvest in my life. *Amen.*

My mantra is:
It's my season of harvest and magic.

White Pumpkins and Magic

A white **pumpkin** symbolizes
new **beginnings**.
An orange one reels in more **joy**.
Place a coin by an apple for more **wealth**,
and for good **health**,
pass a **cinnamon** broom.
There is **magic** in fall,
and it's **easy** to call.
All you have to do is **believe**.

Prayer for the Full Moon

Dear Universe, I ask you to help me release what no longer serves my greatest and highest good on this Full Moon. I am ready to ebb and flow to the abundance you have for me and the intentions nestled in my heart.
I use this ritualistic format:
"I release x energy and invite in x abundance."
Thank you for my blessings. I know this Full Moon is a turning point in my life as it closes out a cycle. I accept the truths I need to see now and bravely take action towards my authentic desires. I trust in the mystery of how my intentions will arrive. *Namaste.*

My mantra is:
I glow like the moon.

To Feel, To Be Real

Just like the Full **Moon**,
I move in **phases**.
I **shine** bright.
I allow myself to **feel** and
be real with who I am and what I **desire**.
The expanding emotions **rising**
within my **heart**
tell me I need to **let** go
of what no longer serves **me**.
I now **open** the **door** to
what I truly **deserve**.

Prayer for Mercury Retrograde

Dear Universe, help me navigate this Mercury Retrograde phase with peace and patience. Remind me to trust that, if there are delays, they are in my favor. Assist me in reconnecting with old beautiful friends and cultivating family time. Illuminate me in what old projects deserve to be completed and what ways I can improve my life. I love my growth during this time. Thank you, Universe, for guiding me during this transformative time into my butterfly era. *Namaste.*

My mantra is:
I am in my butterfly era.

Annie Vazquez

Butterflies are Born

Mercury Retrograde is my **caterpillar** stage,
where I enter my **cocoon** for a few weeks.
Here, I self-reflect, **transform**
and allow myself to be
reborn into my **butterfly** era.

Prayer for the New Moon

Dear Universe, thank you for this New Moon. I honor this beautiful fresh energy in my life. It inspires me to be brave and take chances, to start something new and continue to follow what calls my heart. When I show up for myself, the Universe shows up for me and my dreams actualize. I use the words "I am grateful for" with my intentions as if they have already happened. Thirty days from today, I witness my intentions manifesting. Thank you, Universe, for helping me co-create in this brand New Moon cycle. *Namaste.*

My mantra is:
New Moon, new me.

Glow Again

There's a new version of me **emerging**.
I can't see her yet like the New **Moon**
that's dark in the **sky**,
but soon, she and **I** will
glow again.
That's how new **beginnings** begin.

Prayer for Spring Equinox

Dear Universe, thank you for this new season of fertility and growth. I am elated to notice flowers sprouting from the earth and my intentions blossoming. I am grateful to see newborn animals coming into the world and me, witnessing my rebirth, too. I am ecstatic for warmer weather and longer days of light. I prepare for this fresh start and abundance. I spring clean my space by decluttering, donating items I no longer use and tossing out broken ones. I decorate with flowers, like tulips, burn incense to purify my home with the windows open and sprinkle cinnamon by the doorway for abundance to come knocking. *Amen.*

My mantra is:
I blossom this spring.

Sweet Spring

A **season** of fertility and expansion,
warmer breezes and longer days of **light**,
a strawberry Full Moon **signaling** the
sweetness of all the freshness blooming.
Tulips, butterflies and **nature's**
newborns **move** about with their mothers.
Spring cleaning purifies the past
while a **dash** of cinnamon at the door
brings in future **abundance**.

Prayer for Summer Solstice

Dear Universe, thank you for this season of light. I welcome this time by basking in nature. I am grateful to work with the yang energy and fire element the next three months. The season's sunshine cleanses my aura, ignites my solar plexus and brings me more courage and confidence. The fire energy propels my intentions to move faster. I reel in my limitless power by using citrine. I place this crystal on my intentions and on my belly. I ignite the magic of this season in my home with sunflowers, marigolds or yellow daisies. I enjoy lemons, oranges, grapefruits and other sun-colored fruits to further engage the power of this marvelous season. I light candles envisioning my goals coming to fruition and I am blessed. *Amen.*

My mantra is:
My intentions are ignited this summer.

Annie Vazquez

A Season of Light

A season of **light** is running towards us.
3 months to **bask** outdoors and
slow **dance** in fields of
sunflowers, marigolds and yellow daisies.
Plenty of time to make **fresh** orange marmalade
for crunchy **morning** toast and eat grapefruits in bikinis.
Yellow citrine **sparkling** in hand,
we are reminded we are **gems** too
and we **deserve** to shine
this **summer**.

Prayer for Winter Solstice

Dear Universe, thank you for this season of darkness and rebirth. I welcome this transformative time by becoming more introspective and recharging indoors. I am grateful to honor the natural cycle of the earth for the next three months. Snow is full of magic. I hold it in my hands, set an intention with it, cast it into the sky with laughter and it is granted. I find the magic of winter by releasing what needs to go and celebrating the slow return to the light. I create space in my home by bringing in mistletoe, poinsettias and twinkling lights. I enjoy warm meals and beverages. I light cozy cinnamon and pine-scented candles, envisioning my goals coming to fruition. I am blessed this season. *Amen.*

My mantra is:
This is my rebirth.

Winter Magic

A season of darkness and **rebirth**.
3 months to make a **transformation** back
into the light.
A natural **cycle** to let go of what feels heavy
and **celebrate** life by
playing in the snow and using it for **magic**,
decorating with mistletoe, poinsettias and
twinkling **lights**,
relishing warm soups, ciders, spices
and the **romance** of cozy lighting
with cinnamon and pine **candles**.

Angels

Your Guardian Angel

All of us have a Guardian Angel that is assigned to us at the time of our birth. This angel's job is to look after you and guide you throughout your lifetime. Your angel wants to communicate and assist you with your wishes. Praying, speaking or writing them a letter explaining what you'd like them to help you with are some ways to connect. Our Guardian Angels love us very much and want to see us happy.

Guardian Angel Prayer

Dear Guardian Angel, I ask you to protect me, my space and my loved ones now. I can feel your golden light wrapping us in your protection energy. I know that every time I call onto you for assistance on a certain matter, you support me and bring me the guidance I need. When I need extra illumination on a something, I know that if I light a candle for you and ask you for this wisdom, you will show me the way. Today, I ask you for peace and a sign on this matter. I know that you have been with me since birth, looking after me and I want to thank you for all you do to help me. *Namaste.*

My mantra is:
My Guardian Angel always guards me.

Your Guardian Angel

A **Guardian** Angel greeted you in the delivery room
when you were born into this **world** and
told you it was here to protect, **guide**
and **love** you unconditionally in this life and
whenever you needed **help**.
When was the last time you spoke to your **angel**?

Angels And How They Can Help You

Ariel: Aids with animals and plants.

Azrael: Helps souls transition to their next life and comforts those who are grieving.

Cassiel: Aids in protecting you from psychic attacks, protects property and assists with long-term goals.

Chamuel: Brings you healthy loving relationships and marriage.

Gabriel (The Celestial Messenger): Helps resolve problems and brings you soul purpose and pregnancy.

Haniel: Brings joy and connects you to the moon.

Jeremiel: Encourages you to forgive and release resentment so you can open yourself to blessings.

Jophiel: Helps you pass exams, become creative and see the beauty in the world.

Metatron: Connects you with the Merkabah and can clear low energy and help you understand the Universe.

Michael (The Celestial Warrior): Provides protection.

Raphael (The Celestial Healer; The Universe's Physician): Helps doctors with surgery, and also helps you travel.

Sandalphon: Assists musicians and composers, and protects the unborn. This angel will bring you songs to guide you.

Samael: Guides you from wrong and right, and offers you healing.

Zadkiel: Encourages you to transmute your energy to prosperity and freedom.

Angel Numbers

111: New beginnings + tuning in with your spiritual side.

222: Surrender to the flow + trust the process. New opportunities.

333: Encouragement. Time to make essential changes.

444: Release doubts + keep moving forward in faith.

555: Major life changes are manifesting.

666: Re-examine your life + get into a better alignment.

777: Self-awareness has increased. A break-through will occur soon.

888: Abundance is materializing

999: Forgiveness. Release control + accept the reality of a certain situation. End of a chapter.

1010: Everything is working out for you. Moving towards higher purpose.

1111: Make wishes. We all are one. Keep your mind optimistic as what we think, we become.

1212: Luck in love. Obstacles are being removed.

Annie's Favorite Angel Prayers

Prayer to Archangel Ariel

Dear Archangel Ariel, thank you for helping heal the earth and take care of animals. I am grateful that you clean waters, strengthen plants and keep animals safe. I ask you to open my heart and show me how to give back to Mother Earth. I know that you are connected with the direction of the North and guide many with their destiny and new beginnings. Please enlighten me and show me the way. I am ready to be guided and receive your messages. Lastly, I know that you aid us in recovering missing items and people. Please bring back anything that I lost and need to find again. *Amen.*

My mantra is:
Animals and Mother Earth are healing,
thanks to Archangel Ariel.

When to Pray to Archangel Ariel

Archangel Ariel is the **protector** of the **natural world**. Pray to Ariel when Mother Earth needs help. You can call on this angel to **aid** a **plant** or **animal** that is injured. This angel cares about the welfare of the community. Ariel can also help you **find** any **missing item** or person as well as **guide** you to your **destiny**.

Prayer to Archangel Chamuel

Dear Archangel Chamuel, thank you for keeping my relationships healthy and happy. I ask you to balance my heart chakra and align me with pure love, peace and emotional balance. I feel your pink ray of light cleansing my spirit and opening me to receive love. I am grateful that you inspire me to forgive and let go of resentment. I feel pain, hurt and disappointments melting off my body. I am now liberated and open to receive more love and abundance. Chamuel, I feel my self-esteem and self-love blossoming. Lastly, Chamuel, bring me romance and a healthy loving partnership that leads to a beautiful marriage. *Amen.*

My mantra is:
I am love and love surrounds me,
thanks to Archangel Chamuel.

When to Pray to Archangel Chamuel

Archangel Chamuel is known as one of the **romance angels**. Pray to Chamuel when you need **guidance** in romance, partnerships and emotional **balance**. This angel can **heal** your **heart** chakra, help you forgive and have **self-love**. If you are single, Chamuel can bring you **marriage**.

Prayer to Archangel Gabriel

Dear Archangel Gabriel, thank you for helping me tackle my situation and make positive decisions. I am grateful that you bring me options to resolve my situation. I am open and ready for the changes you have for my best and highest self. I know that you illuminate many in finding their purpose and soul mission. I ask you to help me with my purpose and show me what I need to do. I feel my throat chakra clearing now and opening to receive your divine messages. *Amen.*

My mantra is:
I resolve all, thanks to Archangel Gabriel.

When to Pray to Archangel Gabriel

Archangel Gabriel is the **Angel of the Mind**. Call on Gabriel when you need **assistance** making a **decision**. He will **bring** you **options** to reach a solution. Archangel Gabriel is synonymous with change, communication skills and **finding** your **life purpose** and **soul mission**. Gabriel can also help you with **pregnancy**. He is known to **help** with **fertility**, childbearing and adoption.

Prayer to Archangel Michael

Dear Archangel Michael, thank you for the protection you bring me. I ask you to bestow your holy shield around me. Please guard me and my life now. Slay any negative energies that are trying to cause me harm. Slay the demons and temptations that are trying to lure me and bring ill into my life. Give me strength and courage to overcome my challenges and fears. Protect me from evil eyes and return any bad energy to sender with peace and light. If I have any darkness or blocks on me now, I ask you to break these chains. I trust in your guidance and in the detours and delays you bring me now for protection. *Amen.*

My mantra is:
I am safe and protected with Archangel Michael.

When to Pray to Archangel Michael

Archangel Michael is a **heavenly warrior** and **protector**. Pray to him for protection for yourself and your **loved ones**. Call on him any time you feel temptation leading you astray from your goals or if you feel weak. He will come to you immediately and you will feel his **beautiful healing energy**.

Prayer to Archangel Raphael

Dear Archangel Raphael, thank you for my well being. I know you are the Universe's angel physician. I am grateful that you come to me and my loved ones, and look after our health when I call on you. It gives me great confidence to know that you are by our side. I can feel your protection. During health check ups or procedures, I ask you to guide the doctors and nurses so that everything works out in my favor. With my travel, please watch over me and guide me from point A to B for a safe arrival and departure. *Amen.*

My mantra is:
I am healthy and travel safely,
thanks to Archangel Raphael.

When to Pray to Archangel Raphael

Archangel Raphael is known to **heal** ailments from the **physical** and **mental body**. He also **helps travelers**, those having meetings and doctors and nurses. Pray to him for your **well-being**. If you or a loved one has a surgery, ask him to look over it and help the nurses and doctors. If you are embarking on a trip, ask Raphael to be with you. If you have a **special meeting**, ask Raphael to assist you with it.

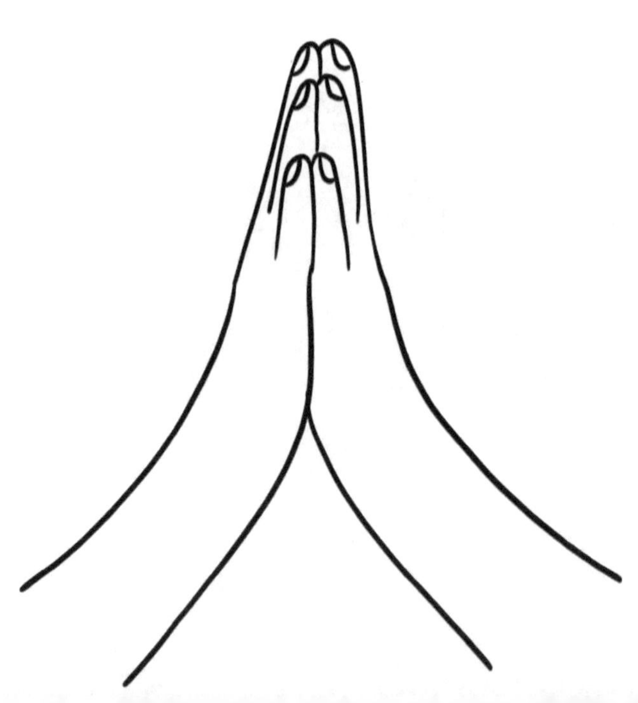

Prayer Request

Go back to the **page** where you wrote what **prayers** you needed **answered**. Know that the **Universe** has read this page and many of your prayers were answered or are currently **manifesting**.

Final Thoughts

Always Remember That...

Everything is working out for you.
All you need to do is pray.
Ask the Universe for guidance.

Your Prayers Are Answered...

Your prayers are always answered
with a "yes,"
"I have something better for you" or a
"be patient,
it's arriving in divine time."

Things Are Falling Into Place...

If you think things feel like they are falling apart,
they are actually falling into place.
Trust everything is working out for you.
It's going to turn out better than you expected.
All you need to do is ask the Universe for guidance and pray.
The direction you seek will be shown to you.

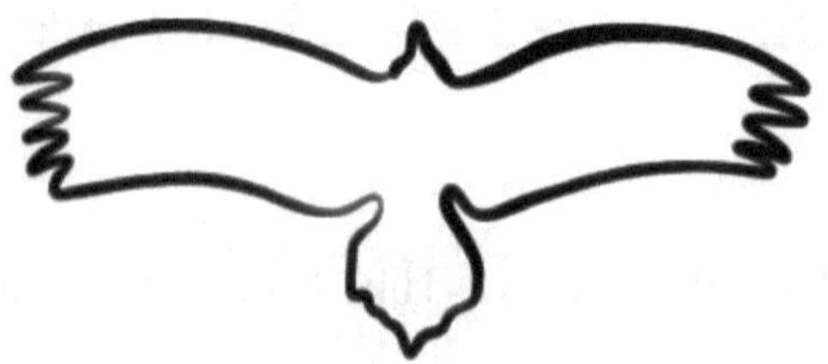

Immediate Angelic Assistance...

In 911 emergencies,
you can prayer-speed-dial Archangel Michael,
your Guardian Angel or an ancestor,
and they can work fast miracles for you.

Make Your Life A Moving Prayer...

Make your life a moving prayer.
Every morning when you wake up, pray for yourself,
for those around you and those you might never meet but need a prayer.
Your prayers have a magnitude that can move mountains.

Signs from Above...

Feathers are the Universe's form of reminding you
that your angels are always with you,
ready to hear you and help you.

My Little Prayer Book

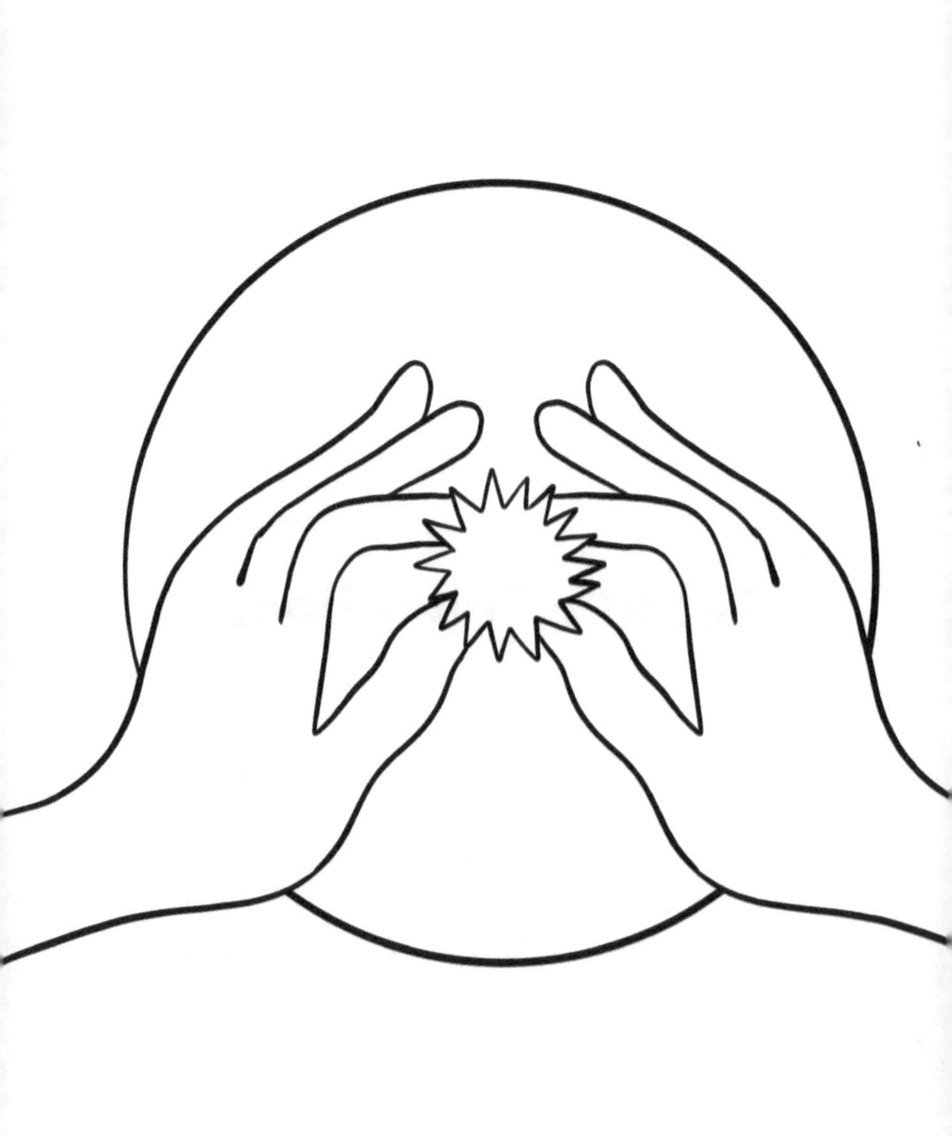

Leave A Review:

I would love to know your thoughts on how *My Little Prayer Book* helped you or someone you care about. Leave me a review so we can connect further and so we can continue to inspire others to believe in the power of prayer.

Acknowledgments

I would like to thank my heroes, **George** and **Carmen**,
for their pure love, continual inspiration and for believing in me.
I love you both infinitely.

My family for showing me how powerful prayer is and how it is our faith
that leads us through storms and up mountains.
I have fond memories of my **Tia Abuela** praying with a rosary,
and statues of saints peppering her home as well as my **grandparents** with
their framed painting of *The Last Supper*.

I want to thank **Elmo** for his loyalty and cute little snores
and nudges to take a break, go for a walk and come back to write.

Petunia, thank you for helping me finish this book and cheering me on
every day.

Annie The Alchemist followers for your energy, kindness,
our prayer circles and for asking me to make this prayer book for us.

My spiritual teachers and friends **Natasha Esteban** and **Carol Ward**
for your nourishing guidance.

Breonna Rodriguez, I am forever grateful to you, *hermana cósmica*. Thank
you for your inspiring talks and your beautiful friendship.

My friends for believing in my creative ideas and cheering me on.

Flor Ana for being the best mentor, editor and *amiga*,
and holding my hand through the entire process
with so much light and love.

Indie Earth Publishing for helping me put this out into the world.

All the **readers** who find light in these pages.

Annie Vazquez's poetry
has also been featured in:

The Spell Jar: Poetry for the Modern Witch (2022)

Love Letters To The 305 (2023)

Glow: Self-Care Poetry for the Soul (2023)

The Spell Jar: Book of Shadows (2023)

About the Author

Annie Vazquez is a poet, writer and former journalist, featured in the Miami Herald, Refinery29, NBC6 and Good Morning America. Annie is known for pioneering Miami fashion blogging through her award-winning blog The Fashion Poet, which has been seen in countless glossies, like Vogue Brasil. Brands like Mercedes Benz, American Express, Coach, H&M, Veuve Cliquot and several tourism boards are just a few that have hired her. Her other brainchild, Annie the Alchemist, is an online wellness shop that offers tools and meditations, reiki and sound bowl healing. Annie is certified by Deepak Chopra's Chopra Meditation School, and her shop has been featured on People Español, Elite Daily, Latin Biz, Parents and Time Out Magazine. Annie has published a variety of ebooks on self-love and wellness and has created a bestselling affirmation deck titled *Affirmations for Abundance.* Her poetry has been featured in a variety of anthologies and publications, including *The Spell Jar: Poetry for the Modern Witch* and *Glow: Self-Care Poetry for the Soul,* among others. When Annie is not writing, she is hanging out with her BFFs, Elmo and Petunia, and traveling the world.

Connect with Annie on Instagram:
@anniewriteswords / @thefashionpoet / @anniethealchemist

www.annievazquez.com

About Indie Earth Publishing

Indie Earth Publishing is an author-first, independent co-publishing company based in Miami, FL. A publisher for writers founded by a writer, Indie Earth offers the support and technical assistance of traditional publishing to writers without asking them to compromise their creative freedom. Each Indie Earth Author is a part of an inspired and creative community that only keeps growing. For more titles from Indie Earth, or to inquire about publication, visit:

indieearthbooks.com.

Instagram: @indieearthbooks

For inquiries, please email:
indieearthpublishinghouse@gmail.com